I. Introduction

Anxieties about the declining influence of U.S. banks in international markets made headlines, and prompted Congressional inquiries, in the late 1980s and early 1990s. More recently, however, concern about U.S. banks' competitiveness overseas has given way to alarm about the growing market share of foreign banks in U.S. markets.[1] By one estimate, foreign banks now hold nearly 50 percent of all existing commercial and industrial loans made to U.S. businesses. Moreover, foreign banks made these gains swiftly, more than doubling their share of the U.S. market in the past 10 years.[2]

Conceptually, a firm can increase its market share by charging lower prices than its rivals and/or by producing higher quality products and services than its rivals. There is some empirical evidence that foreign banks may have employed both strategies, underpricing U.S. banks in some types of loans and offering higher quality service than U.S. banks in some product lines.[3] In competitive markets, these strategies will reduce profits – low price strategies reduce per unit revenues, and high quality strategies increase per unit costs – unless they generate higher unit sales or allow the bank to charge higher prices. Consistent with this, low profitability has been a chronic problem for foreign banks operating in the U.S.[4]

---

[1] Concerning the competitiveness of U.S. banks abroad, see "International Competitiveness of U.S. Financial Institutions," Hearings before the Subcommittee on Financial Institutions Supervision, Regulation and Insurance, (1990); and LaFalce, "Report of the Task Force on the International Competitiveness of U.S. Financial Institutions," (1990). Concerning the inroads made by foreign banks in the U.S., see Fred R. Bleakley, "U.S. Banks Lose Corporate Clients To Lenders Abroad," *The Wall Street Journal* (Sept. 29, 1992); James R. Kraus, "Foreign Banks Control 45% of Corporate Loans in U.S.," *American Banker* (June 15, 1992); and James R. Kraus, "Estimate of Foreign Bank Lending in U.S. Raised," *The Washington Post* (June 16, 1992).

[2] Nolle (1995).

[3] See Calomiris and Carey (1994) and Greenwich Associates (1988, 1992).

[4] See discussion in Section II of this paper.

A third, and perhaps more obvious, explanation for low profits at foreign banks is cost inefficiency. Three recent studies lend credence to this possibility. Employing a stochastic cost frontier framework, Chang, Hasan, and Hunter (1994) conclude that subsidiaries of foreign banks operating in the U.S. have been less cost-efficient than U.S.-owned multinational banks over the past decade. Nolle (1995) reaches a similar conclusion, based on the results from a thick cost frontier model estimated by DeYoung (1993). Using non-parametric methods, Elyasiani and Mehdian (1993) find higher, but not statistically significant, levels of cost inefficiency in foreign-owned banks. However, each of these studies measures cost efficiency only, and ignores the possibility that foreign-owned banks might have offset their relatively large cost inefficiencies with revenue efficiencies. This would be the case if foreign-owned banks produced higher quality products and services than did U.S. banks, and thus generated greater sales at any given price.

This study investigates the relative profit efficiency of foreign-owned U.S. banks and U.S.-owned banks between 1985 and 1990, a period during which foreign bank market share was expanding rapidly. We employ a profit frontier model similar to the one pioneered by Berger, Hancock, and Humphrey (1993) that allows us to estimate both input (cost) and output (revenue) inefficiencies. This allows a more comprehensive analysis than in previous cost efficiency approaches, which do not account for interbank differences in output efficiency. In addition, we modify the Berger, Hancock, and Humphrey model so that it is less sensitive to asset size, includes a greater percentage of bank output, and controls for portfolio and financial risk.

Our results suggest that U.S. subsidiaries of foreign banks were significantly less profit efficient than U.S.-owned banks. Although there was little difference between the two sets of banks in terms of output efficiency, foreign-owned banks had a distinct disadvantage in terms of input efficiency, a disadvantage primarily driven by excess expenditures on purchased funds. The results imply that foreign-owned banks placed growth ahead of profitability, and may have allowed loan growth to outstrip their ability to develop the relationships necessary to grow their base of core deposits.

II. Market Share and Performance of Foreign Banks in the U.S.

For the most part, foreign banks that operate in the U.S. can be classified either as subsidiaries (subs) of their home country parent bank, or as branches or agencies (B&As) of their home country parent bank.[5] Foreign-owned subsidiaries are separately capitalized, full-service banks with U.S. bank charters. Foreign-owned branches are not separately capitalized, but can accept deposits and have full banking powers, whereas foreign-owned agencies generally cannot accept deposits and are more limited in the banking services they can provide. Figures 1 and 2 show the growth in the number and assets of subs and B&As in the U.S. from 1983 through the second quarter of 1993.

A. Market Share

The share of commercial and industrial (C&I) loans to U.S. businesses held by foreignbanks increased dramatically between 1983 and 1993. This surge in C&I loans is

---

[5] Foreign banks can also operate Edge Act corporations, Agreement corporations, investment companies, and representative offices. Each of these organizational forms entails significant restrictions on banking activities, and together they account for only a small portion of foreign-owned banking assets in the U.S. See Key and Welsh (1988), Houpt (1988), Damanpour (1991), Lund (1993), Jackson (1993), and Aguilar (1995) for detailed descriptions of the types and amounts of foreign banking activities in the U.S.

documented in Figure 3. By conventional measures, foreign banks' market share more than doubled over this period, from 14 percent to 32 percent. These figures are based on a narrow market definition that includes only onshore lending by foreign banks to U.S. firms (i.e., loans booked at U.S. offices of foreign banks). McCauley and Seth (1992) argue that including offshore lending by foreign banks to U.S. firms (i.e., loans booked at non-U.S. offices of foreign banks) more accurately represents the influence of foreign banks in the U.S. market. Using data on external lending from the Bank for International Settlements (BIS), McCauley and Seth estimated offshore lending to U.S. businesses by foreign banks, and added this amount to the onshore lending. When this broader market definition is used in Figure 3, foreign banks account for 47 percent of C&I loans to U.S. businesses in 1993.

There are a number of possible explanations for the increased presence of foreign banks in U.S. loan markets. Perhaps the most popular is that foreign banks have "followed" clients from their home countries into U.S. markets. Foreign business firms have engaged in a growing volume of international trade with, and direct investment into, the U.S. over the past decade. Hultman and McGee (1989), Budzeika (1991), and Grosse and Goldberg (1991) all show that foreign banks entered the U.S. market to service the international trade and direct investment needs of their home-country clients. However, Terrell (1993, p. 913) notes that, once in the U.S., "many foreign banks have expanded their customer base by actively soliciting business from U.S. companies." Terell's conclusion is reenforced by Seth and Quijano (1991, 1993), who find a diminishing link between trade and direct investment flows from Japan into the U.S., and the growth of Japanese-owned banks in the U.S.

There are other explanations of foreign banking in the U.S. that either complement or extend the "follow the customers" theory.[6] Grubel (1977), Gray and Gray (1981), Rugman and Kamath (1987), and Casson (1990) hypothesize that the possession of firm-specific advantages allow banks to operate successfully abroad. Hultman and McGee (1989) find a positive relationship between the foreign exchange value of the dollar and foreign banking expansion into the U.S. market. Cooper, et al. (1989) show that this result holds more strongly for banks from Pacific-Rim nations than for banks from Western European countries. Goldberg and Saunders (1981) find that interest rate differentials between U.S. and foreign deposits and loans, price/earnings ratios of U.S. bank stocks, expectations of changes in banking regulations, levels of direct foreign investment, and exchange rates were all significant determinants of the growth of foreign banks in the U.S. Bartholomew and Galbraith (1990) suggest that the enactment of regional trade agreements could lead to an increase in direct investment in banking; however, three years after the enactment of the Cananda-U.S. Free Trade Agreement, Bartholomew, Binhammer, and Kolinski (1992) find little evidence of greater U.S./Canada banking integration. Goldberg and Grosse (1994) find that differences in state banking laws affect the location and growth decisions of foreign banks.

Once foreign banks are established in the U.S., they can increase their presence either by expanding internally, by purchasing assets from U.S. banks, or by purchasing other banks. Calomiris and Carey (1994) show that foreign banks have gained market share mainly by purchasing existing loans, rather than by originating new loans. For foreign banks that are relatively new to U.S. financial markets, and have few existing relationships with U.S. borrowers, purchasing loans in the secondary market provides one avenue for rapid growth.

---

[6]See Goldberg (1992, pp. 175-178) for a selected review of this literature.

Acquiring existing banks is another way to grow quickly without having to originate new loans, and some foreign banks have used this strategy to expand in the U.S.[7]

There is mixed evidence that foreign banks' recent success in U.S. markets have been aided by cost advantages relative to U.S.-owned banks. Zimmer and McCauley (1991) estimated the average spreads on loans to U.S. corporations necessary to cover the cost of bank capital backing such loans. They concluded that banks from a number of countries enjoyed a cost of capital advantage over U.S. banks between 1984 and 1990. This advantage ranged from 68 basis points for subsidiaries of Japanese banks to 6 basis points for subsidiaries of U.K. banks. Goldberg (1982, p. 144) found conflicting evidence, and concluded that between 1976 and 1979, "...on a total cost of funds basis, U.S. subsidiaries of foreign banks appear to have no comparative cost advantage over their domestic peers."

Until recently, U.S. branches and agencies of foreign banks enjoyed some regulation-based cost advantages. Prior to 1991, B&As could avoid Federal Reserve Eurocurrency reserve requirements by booking loans to U.S. borrowers at offshore offices, and prior to the implementation of the Basle Accord in 1988, cross-country differences in bank capital requirements may have reduced the cost of capital for B&As operating in the U.S.[8] Apart from regulatory advantages, both McCauley and Seth (1992) and Terrell (1993) suggest that offshore B&As may have a lower cost of funds than U.S. banks due to their ability to raise deposit funds outside U.S. markets.

---

[7] See Kraus (1995).

[8] See Frankel and Morgan (1992). Wagster, Cooper, and Kolari (1994) find evidence that, even after the Basle Accord went into effect, differences among countries in their implementation of the agreement resulted in differences in the cost of capital for banks.

To the extent that they existed, cost advantages could have allowed foreign banks to gain U.S. market share by underpricing U.S.-owned banks. Calomiris and Carey (1994) show that, over the 1986-1993 period, foreign-owned banks underpriced U.S.-owned banks by between 25 and 42 basis points on loans to investment-grade firms. Cost advantages also could have helped foreign banks out-compete U.S. banks on the basis of service quality. A survey by Greenwich Associates (1988) showed that, in the late 1980s, U.S. corporate borrowers increasingly turned to foreign banks from a variety of countries because of quality-of-service factors. Canadian, British, and Swiss banks were cited as offering a "reliable source of credit," while German and Far Eastern banks were cited for their "international service capabilities."[9] The same survey showed that Japanese, French, and Dutch banks were most highly regarded for "competitive loan pricing."

B. Performance

Given their supposed cost advantages, it should have been possible for foreign banks to maintain profits roughly in line with those earned by U.S.-owned banks, while at the same time underpricing U.S. banks, producing higher quality services than U.S. banks, or some combination of both. However, both Seth (1992) and Nolle (1995) find profit rates at foreign-owned banks operating in the U.S. lagged behind profit rates for U.S.-owned banks during the past decade. For every year but 1987 (when U.S. money center banks provisioned for problem loans to LDCs), these studies concluded that return on assets (ROA) and return on

---

[9] See Greenwich Associates (1988, p. 4). The report also noted "three key reasons" why "foreign banks are used more than money center and regional banks" (p. 4). These reasons were competitive loan pricing, international service capabilities, and proposing innovative international banking alternatives. A more recent report (Greenwich Associates, 1992, p. 2) notes an increase in the "number of U.S. companies reporting that foreign banks propose innovative banking alternatives."

equity (ROE) at foreign banks were less than that for a cohort group of otherwise similar U.S. banks.[10]

Three recent studies suggest that cost inefficiency provides an explanation for the low profitability of foreign-owned U.S. banks. Chang, Hasan, and Hunter (1994) estimate a stochastic cost frontier model for a panel of foreign-owned and U.S.-owned multinational banks operating with U.S. charters between 1984 and 1989. In regressions that control for asset size, bank holding company form, and non-U.S. lending activity, the authors find that cost inefficiency is positively related to foreign ownership. Nolle (1995) performs a univariate comparison and finds similar results. Using annual estimates of cost inefficiencies from DeYoung (1993) that are derived from a thick cost frontier model, Nolle concludes that the average foreign-owned sub was less cost efficient than the average U.S. bank in every year but one between 1984 and 1992. In a third study, Elyasiani and Mehdian (1992) use data envelopment analysis to measure cost efficiency for a sample of foreign-owned and U.S.-owned U.S. banks in 1988. The authors find that foreign-owned banks were less efficient than U.S.-owned banks, although this difference was not statistically significant.

III. Profit Efficiency

Cost efficiency models assume that banks take current input prices and output quantities as given, then seek to minimize costs by hiring the optimal levels of inputs. As such, any inefficiencies estimated using these models must be attributed exclusively to hiring an excess amount, or a suboptimal mix, of inputs. However, a bank might also be inefficient

---

[10] Because B&As are not required to file income data on their call reports, these studies estimated the income components of ROA and ROE using Commerce Department data. To estimate ROE, the implied equity position of parent banks in their B&As also had to be estimated. See Seth (1992) and Nolle (1995) for details.

if it produces too few, or a non-optimal mix of, outputs given the inputs it employs and the prices that it faces -- i.e., a bank may not be revenue efficient. By not recognizing this possibility, cost-based models may misrepresent the nature and extent of inefficiency in banks. For example, in order to produce above-average service quality, a bank will probably have to hire more and/or more expensive inputs, and as a result may be mistakenly identified as cost-inefficient by a purely cost-based model. Such banks may actually be *profit*-efficient: since the market will demand more of, or pay more for, high service quality, these banks may generate additional revenues large enough to offset their relatively high expenses.

In this section, we present a profit efficiency model designed to generate separate estimates of input (or cost) and output (or revenue) inefficiency for a sample of U.S. subsidiaries of foreign banks and U.S.-owned banks between 1985 and 1990. Our model is a modified version of a profit efficiency model originally introduced by Berger, Hancock, and Humphrey (1993). References to the original paper are held to a minimum, and are limited for the most part to discussing the differences between the two approaches.

A. *Profit Efficiency Model*

We assume that banks seek to maximize variable profits π in the short-run by choosing a vector of variable netputs x, given fixed factors z and a vector of input and output prices p. Hence, banks maximize $\pi = \Sigma\, px$, where netputs are positive for output quantities and negative for input quantities. We specify a quadratic variable profit function as follows:

$$(1) \quad \pi(p,z,\xi)/p_n = \sum_{i=1}^{n} (\alpha_i - \xi_i)(p_i/p_n) + \frac{1}{2}\sum_{i=1}^{n-1}\sum_{j=1}^{n-1} \varphi_{ij}(p_i p_j / p_n^2)$$

$$+ \sum_{r=1}^{k} \beta_r z_r + \frac{1}{2} \sum_{r=1}^{k} \sum_{s=1}^{k} \theta_{rs} z_r z_s + \sum_{i=1}^{n-1} \sum_{r=1}^{k} \gamma_{ir} (p_i/p_n) z_r$$

where *i* indexes the *n* different netputs. Derived netput demands are generated by applying Hotelling's lemma to equation (1):

$$(2) \quad x_i(p,z) = \partial \pi(p,z)/\partial p_i = (\alpha_i - \xi_i) + \sum_{j=1}^{n-1} \varphi_{ij}(p_j/p_n) + \sum_{r=1}^{k} \gamma_{ir} z_r$$

$$(3) \quad x_n(p,z) = \partial \pi(p,z)/\partial p_n = (\alpha_n - \xi_n) - \frac{1}{2} \sum_{i=1}^{n-1} \sum_{j=1}^{n-1} \varphi_{ij}(p_i p_j/p_n^2)$$

$$+ \sum_{r=1}^{k} \beta_r z_r + \frac{1}{2} \sum_{r=1}^{k} \sum_{s=1}^{k} \theta_{rs} z_r z_s$$

Using the *n*th netput price as the numeraire imposes linear homogeneity in prices. Symmetry is imposed by restricting $\theta_{ij} = \theta_{ji}$ and $\varphi_{rs} = \varphi_{sr}$.

The profit function (1) and the netput demands (2) and (3) are actual, not optimal, relationships. Actual netputs and optimal netputs are related by the identity $x_i^* = x_i + \xi_i$, where x^* is the optimal level of each netput, x is the actual level of each netput, and ξ ($\xi > 0$) is the deviation, for whatever reason, of each netput from its optimal level. The ξ_i capture the underproduction of outputs (positive netputs) and the overuse of inputs (negative netputs). A bank with relatively small values for its ξ_i vector is operating close to the efficient profit frontier, given prices and fixed inputs.

Total inefficiency is the loss of profits due to the underproduction and/or the overuse of netputs:

$$(4) \quad INEFF = \pi(p,z,0) - \pi(p,z,\xi) = \sum_{i=1}^{n} \xi_i p_i$$

INEFF can be decomposed into separate measures of inefficiency for each of the *n* netputs. Total output inefficiency can be derived by summing (4) over i = outputs only, and total input inefficiency can be derived by summing (4) for i = inputs only.

B. Model Estimation

Following Berger Hancock and Humphrey (BHH), we made several adjustments to the model (1) - (3) before estimating it. First, random disturbance terms with zero means were added to each equation:

$$(5) \quad \pi(p,z,\xi)/p_n = \sum_{i=1}^{n}(\alpha_i - \xi_i)(p_i/p_n) + \frac{1}{2}\sum_{i=1}^{n-1}\sum_{j=1}^{n-1}\varphi_{ij}(p_i p_j / p_n^2)$$
$$+ \sum_{r=1}^{k}\beta_r z_r + \frac{1}{2}\sum_{r=1}^{k}\sum_{s=1}^{k}\theta_{rs} z_r z_s + \sum_{i=1}^{n-1}\sum_{r=1}^{k}\gamma_{ir}(p_i/p_n)z_r + e$$

$$(6) \quad x_i(p,z,\xi) = (\alpha_i - \xi_i) + \sum_{j=1}^{n-1}\varphi_{ij}(p_j/p_n) + \sum_{r=1}^{k}\gamma_{ir} z_r + v_i$$

Second, note that the *n*th netput equation was removed because it is redundant. Third, the original intercept terms ($\alpha_i - \xi_i$) were replaced by *average* intercept terms ($\alpha_i - \xi_{i,mean}$), where $\xi_{i,mean}$ is the theoretical population mean for ξ_i. The remainders from these substitutions, ($\xi_{i,mean} - \xi_i$), are absorbed into the errors, which become $v_i + (\xi_{i,mean} - \xi_i)$ and $e + (\xi_{n,mean} - \xi_n)$. When these transformed error terms are averaged across time for each bank, the random components v_i and e should converge to zero, leaving only bank-specific information ($\xi_{i,mean} - \xi_i$) and ($\xi_{n,mean} - \xi_n$) in the average error terms. This approach is a direct analog to the "distribution-free" cost frontier methodology introduced by Berger (1993).

Having made these three adjustments, we estimated the parameters of the model using Iterative Seemingly Unrelated Regression techniques. Let $\hat{v}_i$ and $\hat{e}$ represent the resulting average residuals for each bank, and let $\overline{v}_i$ and $\overline{e}$ represent the maximum values for these averages across all banks. Then we calculate the ξ_i as follows:

$$(7a) \quad \xi_i = \overline{v}_i - \hat{v}_i$$

$$(7b) \quad \xi_n = \overline{e} - \hat{e}$$

The bank with the largest average residual $\hat{v}_i$ or $\hat{e}$ is the most efficient bank for netput i, and is assigned a value of zero for ξ_i. The values in (7) are then used to generate the inefficiency estimates in (4). The values $\overline{v}_i$ and $\overline{e}$ define the efficient profit frontier, and the values ξ_i and ξ_n measure the distance from the frontier in terms of underproduction of outputs and/or overuse of inputs.

IV. Modifying the BHH model

We make three modifications to the BHH model. First, we do not decompose profit inefficiency (4) into allocative and technical components. Second, we modify the distribution-free methodology to better remove the influence of outlying residual values. Third, we re-specify the profit function, expanding the variable netput vector x to include a greater percentage of bank assets, and augmenting the fixed factors vector z to control for financial risk, portfolio risk, and non-lending outputs.

A. Technical and Allocative Inefficiency

The BHH model employs non-standard definitions of technical and allocative inefficiency. The authors define allocative inefficiencies as deviations between the *optimal* levels of netputs and the bank's *desired* levels of netputs (i.e., management chooses a suboptimal production plan), and technical inefficiencies as deviations between the bank's *desired* levels of netputs and the *actual* levels of netputs purchased or produced (i.e., management implements its chosen production plan in a suboptimal fashion). To separate the two types of inefficiency, BHH specify variable profits as a function of a set of shadow relative prices, then make the assumption that allocative inefficiencies arise when management chooses variable netputs based on shadow relative prices that misrepresent actual relative prices (i.e., management incorrectly observes relative prices).

Conceptually, these innovations are useful because they allow us yet another way to isolate different causes of inefficiency. In application, however, the model is somewhat unwieldy. To estimate the BHH model, one must constrain the relationships between shadow prices and actual prices to be identical for all banks. While on some levels this assumption is less restrictive than standard approaches -- it lets the data determine the industry-wide "average" relationship between shadow and actual prices, rather than assuming that all banks perceive relative prices correctly -- it remains unlikely that these relationships are the same for all banks.

Because our objective is to compare the profit efficiency of two sets of banks, we choose not to constrain any portion of measured inefficiency to be identical for both sets of banks. Instead, we estimate total inefficiencies (4), but do not attempt to decompose them into technical and allocative components. In effect, our profit model (1)-(3) constrains banks to observe prices correctly, which forces 100 percent of any inefficiency into the ξ_i terms.[11,12] It is important to note that this does not constrain banks to have zero allocative inefficiency – it is possible for a bank to know the optimal netput vector, but still incur both allocative and technical inefficiencies (by standard definitions) in unsuccessful attempts to produce that vector. Because bank efficiency studies generally yield small estimates of allocative inefficiency, any bias in our results is likely to be negligible.[13]

B. Treatment of Outliers

We make two post-estimation adjustments to prevent outlying residuals (e.g., unusually *lucky* banks, or data errors) from defining the efficient frontier, and to avoid unrealistically large estimates of inefficiency for individual banks (e.g., unusually *unlucky* banks, or data errors). First, if one of the ξ_i for any bank exceeded that bank's actual netput average x_i, we set the offending value of ξ_i equal to x_i. This adjustment follows directly from BHH, and imposes a common sense constraint that estimated netput inefficiencies be no larger than the actual amount of those netputs produced or purchased by the bank.

Second, we separated banks into 10 equal-sized groups (deciles) according to their

---

[11] In terms of the BHH model, we constrain all shadow relative prices (the vector of τs) to equal 1, so that desired production plans are identical to the optimal production plans.

[12] It is theoretically possible to estimate BHH's shadow relative prices (the τs) *separately* for U.S. banks and foreign banks by employing a switching technique, in which a new regime is triggered by a foreign- vs. U.S.-ownership dummy. Such an approach would allow separate estimates of allocative inefficiency for the two sets of banks. However, the resulting non-linear model would be even more complex than the original BHH model, which is already very difficult to make converge using non-linear estimation techniques. Because the banking cost literature tends to find small allocative inefficiencies, and because we already capture both allocative and technical inefficiencies in the ξ terms, we opted to set the τs equal to 1, thus trading the chance to decompose the inefficiency estimates for much lower computational costs.

[13] Berger, Hunter, and Timme (1993) discuss the relative magnitudes of allocative and technical inefficiencies in banks.

average asset size during the sample period. Average residuals ($\hat{v}_i$ and/or $\hat{e}$) that were greater than the 95th percentile, or were less than the 5th percentile, of the distributions of average residuals *within each asset decile* were set equal to those threshold values. This procedure improves on a similar truncation procedure used in the BHH model, which constrains average residuals to remain within the 5th and 95th percentiles of the distribution of average residuals for the *entire sample*. Because the moments of the entire sample distribution are dominated by large banks, the BHH procedure truncates large bank residuals frequently, but truncates small bank residuals infrequently, creating a bias in the estimates of inefficiency (4) that overstates estimated inefficiency in small banks relative to large banks. We report the results of both truncation schemes in section VI.

C. Specifying the Profit Function

In the BHH model, banks purchase two variable inputs (deposits and labor) and combine them with two fixed inputs (core deposits and physical capital) to produce two variable outputs (consumer loans and business loans). This pure intermediation approach to modeling profits is simple and straightforward, and it was adopted in part to make a rather complicated model tractable. However, because this specification fails to measure several categories of bank output, the model will overstate inefficiency for banks (particularly large banks) that hire additional labor, funds, and physical capital in order to produce these services.[14] Furthermore, because this specification contains no controls for portfolio risk or financial risk, profit inefficiency may be overstated for banks with risky investment strategies

---

[14] DeYoung (1994) shows that models that omit non-interest income can substantially overstate cost inefficiency in fee-intensive banks.

or financial structures.

We augment the BHH specification in several ways. First, we replace consumer loans and business loans in the vector of variable netputs x with total loans and securities. While our version of the x vector does not distinguish between different types of lending, it does capture a greater percentage of banks' intermediation output. (Note: We also estimate a version of our model that separates loans into business, consumer, and real estate loans. See section VI.) Second, we include non-interest income in the vector of fixed factors z. Technically, this assumes that non-intermediation outputs are fixed in the short-run (i.e., they do not vary with prices), which is clearly not accurate. However, it is impossible to include these activities as a variable netput in x because the data to construct their prices are not available. Finally, we control for financial risk and portfolio risk, respectively, by including equity capital and risk-weighted assets in the vector of fixed factors z.[15] Banks with low levels of equity capital may have to pay higher rates for purchased funds due to perceived risk of default, and banks that hold relatively risky portfolios of assets are more likely to incur loan workout expenses in addition to paying higher deposit rates.

V. Data

Our sample consists of annual observations of 62 U.S. subsidiaries of foreign banks, and 240 U.S.-owned banks located in the same metropolitan statistical areas (MSAs) as those foreign-owned banks, for the period 1985 through 1990. We define a bank to be foreign-

---

[15] Mester (1993) and Hughes and Mester (1994) include equity capital in a cost function framework to control for the cost of financial risk.

owned if at least 25 percent of the entity's stock is owned by foreign persons or institutions in every year from 1980 through 1990. The selection of subsidiaries, rather than branches and agencies, gives us a group of foreign-owned banks which are in general more nearly like U.S.-owned banks than are branches and agencies.[16] In particular, foreign-owned subsidiaries face the same legal and regulatory requirements as do U.S.-owned banks. Hence, any cost advantages enjoyed by these banks is limited to lower costs of capital. Choosing foreign-owned and U.S.-owned banks from the same MSAs ensures as much as possible that both sets of banks faced similar market conditions.

The data set consists of 1,812 annual observations of variable profits; four variable netputs (total loans, securities, purchased funds, and labor); four variable netput prices; two fixed inputs (core deposits and physical capital stock); two risk variables (equity capital and risk-weighted assets); and a measure of non-intermediation output (non-interest income). Variable profit equals interest and fee revenue from loans and securities, minus interest paid on purchased funds and expenses on wages and benefits. Total loans include commercial and industrial loans, real estate loans, consumer loans, and all other loan assets held by the bank. Securities include all securities held by the bank that were not in the bank's trading account. Purchased funds equals time deposits in excess of $100,000, federal funds purchased, demand notes issued to the U.S. Treasury, and other borrowed money. Labor equals the number of full time equivalent (FTE) workers employed by the bank. Core deposits include transactions deposits, money market deposits, and savings deposits. Physical capital stock equals the book

---

[16] In any case, because branches and agencies file a more abbreviated call report than do separately capitalized (U.S.- or foreign-owned) banks, there is insufficient data to estimate inefficiency measures for these banks.

value of the bank's premises and fixed assets. Equity equals common stock, perpetual preferred stock, capital surplus, undivided profits, and cumulative foreign currency translation adjustments. Risk-weighted assets is the sum of each bank's assets, after weighting different types of assets ($0 \leq$ weights ≤ 1) to reflect their riskiness. Non-interest income equals fee income and net gains associated with a variety of activities, including fiduciary activities, services to depositors, foreign exchange transactions, securities trading, credit enhancements, loan servicing, and mutual fund and insurance sales. Each of the variable netputs and all of the fixed factors are averages of beginning-of-year and end-of-year values. Prices were constructed by dividing the annual revenue or expense associated with each variable netput by the annual average for each variable netput.

To be included in the sample, banks had to have been in continual existence from 1980 through 1990. Any bank operating in a state that had unit banking laws at any time during the sample period was excluded from the sample. Banks reporting a non-positive amount of total loans, securities, purchased funds, or core deposits; having less than 20 full time equivalent (FTE) employees; or having physical capital less than $50,000 in any year during the sample period were also excluded. Finally, because netput prices were constructed rather than observed, banks with unrealistically low or high prices in any year during the sample period were excluded from the sample. All financial data were collected from the Reports of Condition and Income (the "call reports"). Information on unit banking states was taken from Amel (1993). Risk-weighted assets were estimated using the procedure developed by Avery and Berger (1991), and were graciously provided by those authors.

A. Descriptive Statistics

Table 1 displays panel means, standard deviations, and medians for the 62 foreign-owned subsidiary banks and the 240 U.S.-owned banks in our sample over the 1985-1990 period. The size distributions of the two samples are skewed away from each other: foreign-owned banks were larger in terms of the median average, but U.S.-owned banks were larger in terms of means.

Foreign-owned subs used fewer employees per dollar of assets than did U.S.-owned banks, but paid them higher wages and benefits. The former result suggests that foreign-owned subs used labor inputs rather efficiently, but this may simply reflect a less labor-intensive business strategy. For example, foreign subs had significantly fewer core deposits (which require the production of depositor services) than did their U.S.-owned counterparts. The latter result is consistent with anecdotal evidence that foreign-owned banks must pay higher wages and benefits to entice senior managers to live abroad.[17]

By relying less on core deposits, foreign-owned subsidiaries had to finance a considerably larger portion of their assets with purchased funds (25 percent versus 15 percent)

---

[17] For example, see "Foreign Banks in America, Challenges and Opportunities," The CBM Group, Inc. (1995). The payment of higher salaries likely extends to senior American managers at foreign-owned banks, to offset the perception (or reality) of reduced opportunity for advancement within the organization.

Table 1
Descriptive Statistics.
Mean and median averages, six annual observations for each bank.

	Foreign-Owned Subs. (62 banks)			U.S.-Owned Banks (240 banks)		
	Mean	Med.	S.D.	Mean	Med.	S.D.
Variable Netputs						
Employees-per-$10M of Assets	5.77	5.44	2.80	7.18[a]	6.83	2.81
Purchased Funds-to-Assets (%)	25.48	21.97	15.35	14.80[a]	12.96	9.16
Loans-to-Assets (%)	58.93	61.44	18.50	61.50[a]	64.19	14.56
Business Loans-to-Loans (%)	41.71	39.51	15.63	27.27[a]	24.98	14.62
Real Estate Loans-to-Loans (%)	34.62	34.30	19.40	46.63[a]	46.85	18.45
Consumer Loans-to-Loans (%)	13.04	10.48	10.58	20.80[a]	17.95	14.53
Securities-to-Assets (%)	16.02	13.95	10.69	19.84[a]	17.81	12.84
Prices						
Price of Labor ($ thousands)	31.60	30.40	7.81	29.06[a]	27.75	7.42
Price of Purchased Funds (%)	8.73	8.18	2.92	8.60	8.11	2.76
Price of Loans (%)	10.49	10.52	1.54	11.30[a]	11.26	1.44
Price of Business Loans*	9.92	9.53	2.95	12.06[a]	11.37	3.82
Price of Real Estate Loans*	10.65	10.70	2.06	10.79	10.71	2.01
Price of Consumer Loans*	13.10	11.83	5.48	11.92[a]	11.59	2.64
Price of Securities (%)	8.04	8.00	1.49	8.24[a]	8.18	1.31
Fixed Factors						
Physical Capital ($ millions)	29.67	6.00	62.50	33.30	2.47	146.8
Core Deposits-to-Assets (%)	38.23	41.04	16.07	52.98[a]	52.83	12.05
Equity-to-Assets (%)	7.69	6.96	3.29	7.25[a]	6.71	2.87
Risk Weighted Assets Ratio (%)	73.57	71.66	21.93	71.43[b]	73.21	16.99
Non-interest Income-to-Net Revenue (%)	19.09	18.26	9.32	18.63	16.26	10.52
Other Characteristics						
Assets ($ billions)	1.99	0.47	4.06	2.40	0.14	10.13
Cash-to-Assets (%)	16.92	11.63	14.00	9.63[a]	8.45	5.29
Non-performing Loans-to-Loans (%)	3.56	2.66	3.31	2.16[a]	1.36	2.47
Return on Assets (%)	0.29	0.48	1.17	0.71[a]	0.96	1.25
Return on Equity (%)	2.33	7.17	24.45	9.99	13.46	147.0

* Due to data limitations, only 143 U.S.-owned banks and 50 foreign-owned subsidiaries were observed for these variables.
[a] and [b] indicate significant difference between means for the foreign-owned subsidiaries and the U.S.-owned banks at the 1 percent and 5 percent levels, respectively, in a two-tailed test.

than did U.S.-owned banks.[18] Although the two sets of banks paid similar rates for purchased funds, this placed foreign-owned banks at a cost of deposited funds disadvantage relative to U.S.-owned banks during the sample period. The differences in financing mix may indicate that foreign-owned banks had difficulty competing for deposits from domestic customers.

As a percentage of assets, foreign-owned subs produced only slightly fewer loans (59 percent versus 61 percent) than did their U.S. counterparts, but the composition of loan portfolios differed substantially between the two sets of banks. Business loans comprised a significantly higher percentage, while real estate loans and consumer loans comprised a significantly lower percentage, of total loans at foreign banks. As with retail deposits, the relatively low level of consumer loans at foreign subs may indicate a lack of competitiveness at attracting U.S. retail customers. The data also suggest that foreign-owned banks invested their non-loan assets less profitably than did U.S.-owned banks, holding fewer of these assets in securities, and substantially more of these assets in cash and bank deposits.[19] The two sets of banks produced similar levels of non-interest income.

On average, foreign-owned subsidiaries earned significantly lower rates on their loan portfolios and securities portfolios than did their U.S. counterparts. The foreign subs charged higher rates on consumer loans, similar rates on real estate loans, and substantially lower rates on business loans, than did the U.S.-owned banks. The lower prices for business loans suggests that foreign banks either underpriced their U.S.-owned competitors in order to gain

---

[18] The average foreign-owned bank in our sample financed less than 1 percent of its assets with funds purchased from, or funds deposited by, foreign governments, corporations, and financial institutions.

[19] The high amount of cash and bank deposits held by foreign-owned subs may reflect a relatively intensive correspondent relationship with their parent banks.

market share, tended to lend to higher quality business customers, or both.

Pre-tax return on assets (ROA) and equity (ROE) for the 62 foreign-owned banks was only about half that for the 240 U.S.-owned banks. Lower accounting profitability for the foreign subs is consistent with a number of the results shown in Table 1. Reliance on purchased funds probably increased overall interest expenditures, and disproportionate investments in low-yielding assets probably depressed revenues. Depending on demand elasticities and loan quality, charging lower prices on business loans also may have reduced interest revenues. Foreign-owned banks had significantly higher levels of non-performing loans, which require additional labor time to process in addition to reducing revenue from loans. Because their risk-weighted asset ratios were similar to those of U.S. banks (higher mean but lower median), the incidence of non-performing loans might be explained by their business-intensive loan mix, or by poor loan underwriting and monitoring.[20] To some degree, foreign banks offset the relative riskiness of their loan portfolios by holding higher levels of equity capital.

VI. Results

Table 2 displays estimates of variable profit inefficiency for the entire sample of 302 banks. Profit inefficiency is expressed two ways: as the weighted average of the ratio of inefficiency to assets (weighted by each bank's share of total assets), and as the weighted average of the ratio of inefficiency to potential variable profits (weighted by each bank's share of total potential variable profits). Potential variable profits are the variable profits that each

---

[20] The risk-weighted asset ratios were similar for both sets of banks because, even though foreign banks held larger amounts of assets in zero-weighted cash balances, U.S. banks held larger amounts of assets in partially weighted real estate loans.

bank would have generated had it been free of inefficiency, and are estimated by adding the dollar value of inefficiency at each bank (equation 4) to the average variable profit earned by each bank over the sample period. Panel A shows estimates from a model that controls for neither risk or fee-based activities, while panel B shows estimates from a model that includes equity, risk-weighted assets, and non-interest income in the vector of fixed factors z. All results are reported using both of the truncation alternatives discussed above: truncating netput residuals uniformly at the 5th and 95th percentiles of their sample distributions, and truncating netput residuals at the 5th and 95th percentiles of their sample distributions within asset deciles.

A. Overall Profit Inefficiency

Estimated profit inefficiency ranged from as much as 12 percent of assets for small banks (less than $100 million in assets) to as little as ½ percent of assets for large banks (over $5 billion in assets). For the large banks, these results are economically reasonable – they imply that a bank with a 1 percent return on assets could increase its ROA to about 1.5 percent by eliminating all input and output inefficiency. For the small banks, however, these results are less believable, implying that small banks could add 12 percentage points to their ROAs by becoming completely efficient. The negative relationship between inefficiency and asset size is consistent with results produced elsewhere.[21] However, there are at least three reasons why the various estimates of profit inefficiency-to-assets in Table 2 overstate actual profit

---

[21] Humphrey (1987) was the first to report a relatively wide unit cost dispersion for small banks, and a number of the cost studies reviewed in Berger, Hunter, and Timme (1993) find that the average small bank is relatively cost inefficient. In studies of profit inefficiency using a model very similar to the one used here, Berger, Hancock, and Humphrey (1993), Zhu, et. al (1994), and Swamy, Akhavein, and Taubman (1994) all produce estimates of inefficiency that decline markedly with bank size.

Table 2
Profit Inefficiency as a Percentage of Assets and Potential Profits.
Assets in millions of dollars. Averages are weighted by shares of assets or potential profits.

	< $100M	$100-500M	$500-$1B	$1-5B	> $5B	all
N	99	122	17	37	27	302
mean assets	$ 58	$ 228	$ 715	$ 2,390	$20,922	$2,315

A. *Two-Output Model without Risk and Non-interest Income:*

% of assets:						
truncation uniform*	12.03%	10.81%	8.03%	5.25%	1.03%	2.16%
truncation by asset decile*	10.32%	8.91%	9.46%	9.13%	4.01%	4.99%
% of potential profits:						
truncation uniform	68.80%	67.69%	62.66%	57.13%	20.36%	34.66%
truncation by asset decile	65.45%	63.22%	66.48%	69.82%	49.92%	55.06%

B. *Two-Output Model with Risk and Non-interest Income:*

% of assets:						
truncation uniform	12.04%	11.15%	7.02%	3.17%	0.57%	1.52%
truncation by asset decile	7.32%	6.32%	6.16%	5.79%	2.59%	3.24%
% of potential profits:						
truncation uniform	68.81%	68.75%	59.67%	44.65%	12.36%	27.18%
truncation by asset decile	57.86%	55.47%	56.33%	59.47%	39.15%	44.29%

* The uniform truncation scheme truncates netput residuals at the 5th and 95th percentiles of each netput's sample-wide distribution. The asset decile truncation scheme truncates netput residuals at the 5th and 95th percentiles of each netput's distribution within each asset decile.

inefficiency.

First, using a uniform set of thresholds to truncate the netput residuals artificially amplifies the relationship between asset size and inefficiency. Note the contrast between the two truncation schemes in panel A. When the uniform truncation scheme is employed, inefficiencies decline from 12.03 percent of assets for small banks to 1.03 percent of assets for large banks. But when netput residuals are truncated within asset deciles, inefficiencies fall along a smaller range, diminishing from 10.32 percent of assets for small banks to 4.01 percent of assets for large banks. Second, controlling for risk and non-interest income substantially reduces the estimates of profit inefficiency. In panel A, where the profit model does not control for these phenomena, overall profit inefficiency ranges from 2.16 percent to 4.99 percent of assets, while in panel B, overall profit inefficiency falls to between 1.52 percent and 3.24 percent of assets. Third, our estimates of variable profit inefficiency are based on profits before taxes and fixed costs, which will naturally be much larger than net income. As a result, standard ROA ratios will naturally be much smaller than the estimates of inefficiency-to-assets shown in Table 2. For the 302 banks in our sample, median net income averaged only about 17 percent of median variable profits – multiplying our estimates of inefficiency-to-assets by 0.17 is a crude way making them somewhat comparable to accounting ROA ratios.

Making all three of these adjustments reduces the estimates of inefficiency-to-assets considerably. Starting with the uniform truncation results in panel A, estimated profit inefficiencies range from 12.03 percent to 1.03 percent of assets. Switching to the alternate truncation scheme reduces inefficiencies to range between 10.32 percent and 4.01 percent of assets. Controlling for risk and non-interest income reduces the range further, to between 7.32 percent and 2.59 percent of assets. Multiplying these endpoints by 17 percent produces a final – though crude – range of 1.22 percent of assets for small banks to 0.44 percent of assets for large banks. Given that average ROA was 0.86 for the banks in our sample, completely eliminating these inefficiencies would increase ROA by about 150 percent for small banks, and by about 50 percent for large banks, figures that seem economically reasonable.

Expressing estimated profit inefficiency as a percentage of potential profits results in economically reasonable magnitudes without the need for crude adjustments. (Our estimates of potential variable profits and our estimates of variable profit inefficiency are both pre-tax, pre-fixed cost measures of income. In addition, both measures are generated by the same empirical model.) As with the estimates of profit inefficiency-to-assets, the estimates of profit inefficiency-to-potential profits are less sensitive to asset size when the netput residuals were truncated within asset deciles, and tend to be smaller when the profit model includes controls for risk and non-interest income. In panel B, the model with these two attributes generated estimates of profit inefficiency that ranged from 58 percent of potential variable profits for small banks to 39 percent of potential variable profits for large banks. Moreover, profit inefficiency-to-potential profits for banks with less than $5 billion of assets ranged in a tight band between 55 percent to 59 percent. These estimates imply that most banks could approximately double their earnings before taxes and fixed expenses by eliminating all input and output inefficiency.

B. *Foreign-Owned Banks versus U.S.-Owned Banks*

Table 3 shows the relationship between profit inefficiency and foreign ownership. All of the estimates in Table 3 are unweighted averages of variable profit inefficiency-to-potential variable profits. Estimates were generated from a profit model that controls for risk and non-interest income, and netput residuals were truncated within asset deciles.

Overall, the results reenforce the conclusions of both Chang, Hasan, and Hunter (1993) and Nolle (1995)/DeYoung (1993), studies which found relatively large amounts of cost inefficiency in foreign-owned banks. The 62 foreign-owned banks incurred input inefficiencies equal to about 30 percent of potential profits, compared to only about 20 percent for the 240 U.S.-owned banks. However, our results go further by suggesting that the major cause of this efficiency difference – and hence, the lower profitability at foreign-owned banks during the late 1980s – was the overuse of purchased funds. On average, foreign-owned banks' excess expenditures on purchased funds equalled almost 18 percent of their potential variable profits, twice as much as at U.S.-owned banks. This difference was statistically significant at the 1 percent level, and was large enough to cause statistically significant differences between the two sets of banks in both input inefficiency and profit inefficiency. Foreign-owned banks were more profit-inefficient than their U.S.-owned counterparts despite being significantly more output-efficient, a result driven by superior efficiency in producing loan outputs. (Although this last result is consistent with foreign banks' market share gains during the period, further analysis (see Table 4) is warranted before drawing any conclusions.)

Overall, the results in the first panel of Table 3 are consistent with the hypothesis that foreign-owned banks sacrificed profitability during the late 1980s and early 1990s in order to increase market share. Whether they grew their operations by originating loans, by purchasing loans, or by acquiring other banks, these banks may have been unable to develop

Table 3
Inefficiencies as Percentages of Potential Profits.
Netput residuals truncated at the 5th and 95th percentiles of their sample distributions within asset deciles. Profit model has two variable outputs (total loans and securities) and includes controls for risk and non-interest income. Averages are unweighted.

	Foreign-Owned	*U.S.-Owned*	*Difference*
all banks:			
total	66.99%	60.04%	6.95%[a]
output	36.36	39.47	-3.11[b]
input	30.63	20.57	10.06[a]
loans	28.41	32.00	-3.59[b]
securities	7.95	7.47	0.48
purchased funds	17.83	8.88	8.95[a]
labor	12.80	11.68	1.12
N	62	240	
less than $500 million:			
total	64.44%	53.41%	11.03%[a]
output	30.66	30.84	-0.18
input	33.78	22.56	11.55[a]
loans	21.02	22.04	-1.02
securities	9.63	8.81	0.82
purchased funds	15.82	8.56	7.26[a]
labor	17.96	14.00	3.96[a]
N	33	188	
$500 million to $5 billion:			
total	62.99%	55.92%	7.07%
output	29.06	31.82	-2.76
input	33.94	24.09	9.85[c]
loans	22.18	23.97	-1.79
securities	6.88	7.85	-0.97
purchased funds	22.83	14.25	8.58[c]
labor	11.10	9.84	1.26
N	23	31	
over $5 billion:			
total	62.87%	62.19%	0.68%
output	39.16	36.47	2.69
input	23.72	25.72	-2.00
loans	33.49	31.52	1.97
securities	5.66	4.95	0.71
purchased funds	13.93	13.90	0.03
labor	9.78	11.81	-2.03
N	6	21	

[a] indicates significance at the 1 percent level in a two-tailed test.
[b] indicates significance at the 5 percent level in a two-tailed test.
[c] indicates significance at the 10 percent level in a two-tailed test.

and maintain the relationships with U.S. customers necessary to attract core deposits.[22]
Foreign-owned banks may have faced a choice: financing growth with expensive purchased funds, or not growing at all.

The last three panels of Table 3 separate the results by asset size. Efficiency differences between U.S.-owned and foreign-owned banks were sharpest among small banks, and some of these differences also extend to relatively large institutions. Foreign-owned banks with less than $500 million in assets made significantly greater amounts of excess expenditures on both purchased funds and labor inputs than did similar size U.S.-owned banks. The labor-related input inefficiency might be traced to the higher wages paid by foreign-owned banks. Foreign-owned banks with between $500 million and $5 billion in assets were also more input-inefficient than their U.S. counterparts, a result of excess expenditures on purchased funds. These differences were significant at only the 10 percent level, but they were similar in magnitude to the results for the smaller banks. There were no significant efficiency differences among banks with greater than $5 billion in assets.[23] As bank size increased, the overall gap in profit efficiency between the two sets of banks closed – not because foreign-owned banks became relatively more profit efficient, but rather because U.S.-owned banks became less profit efficient.

Table 4 displays estimates of inefficiency-to-potential profits from a model with four variable outputs: commercial and industrial loans, real estate loans, consumer loans, and

---

[22] A smaller percentage of the foreign-owned banks (about 10 percent) made acquisitions during the sample period than did the U.S.-owned banks (about 17 percent). Hence, it is unlikely that foreign-owned banks' relative inefficient performance can be traced to merger-induced disruptions.

[23] Comparisons in this size class are questionable given the instability of the profit model for the largest size classes of banks.

securities. Although this variant of the model has more output categories, it actually contains less information because some types of loans (e.g., loans to foreign governments, loans to other financial institutions, and loans to finance agricultural production) were left out. In addition, a number of banks had to be excluded because they held zero amounts of one or more of the three loan outputs, which made constructing prices for these outputs impossible. Overall, the results are similar to those generated by the two-output model: foreign-owned banks wasted a significantly larger percentage of their potential profits on purchased funds than did U.S.-owned banks, which, together with higher excess expenditures on labor inputs, overwhelmed a slight output efficiency advantage to result in significantly greater profit inefficiency. The small output efficiency advantage held by foreign-owned banks emanated from an advantage in real estate lending. This implies that the real estate portions of foreign banks' loan portfolios generated relatively large amounts of revenue per dollar of loans. However, it is not clear whether this was a result of better underwriting and monitoring, a different mix of real estate loans (commercial versus home mortgages), or whether fast-growing foreign-owned banks simply avoided economic downturns by entering real estate markets after U.S.-owned banks did.

VII. Conclusions

Despite making significant inroads into U.S. loan markets during the past decade, foreign-owned banks have been consistently less profitable than their U.S. competitors. This study investigates whether U.S. subsidiaries of foreign banks experienced input inefficiencies or output inefficiencies that would have resulted in low profits during this time period. We

Table 4
Inefficiencies as Percentages of Potential Profits.
Netput residuals truncated at the 5th and 95th percentiles of their sample distributions within asset deciles. Profit model has four variable outputs (business loans, consumer loans, real estate loans, and securities) and includes controls for risk and non-interest income.

	Foreign-Owned	_U.S.-Owned_	_Difference_
all banks:			
total	70.79%	60.72%	10.07%[a]
output	37.94	40.83	-2.89[b]
input	32.85	19.89	12.96[a]
business loans	10.57	10.03	0.54
real estate loans	12.46	15.83	-3.37[a]
consumer loans	6.44	7.07	-0.63
securities	8.47	7.90	0.57
purchased funds	19.34	8.41	10.93[a]
labor	13.50	11.48	2.02[b]
N	50	143	

[a] indicates significance at the 1 percent level, in a two-tailed test.
[b] indicates significance at the 5 percent level, in a two-tailed test.

estimate a modified version of the profit efficiency model introduced by Berger, Hancock, and Humphrey (1993) that is less sensitive to asset size, measures a greater percentage of bank output, and controls for portfolio and financial risk. Estimating both input (cost) inefficiencies and output (revenue) inefficiencies allows a more comprehensive analysis than previous cost efficiency approaches.

We find that U.S. subsidiaries of foreign banks were significantly less profit-efficient than U.S.-owned banks between 1985 and 1990, a result that was driven by significantly worse input efficiency. That is, given the fixed inputs that both sets of banks employed, the market prices that both sets of banks faced, and the variable outputs that both banks produced, foreign-owned U.S. banks spent more on inputs than did U.S.-owned banks. The difference in input inefficiency stems primarily from foreign-owned banks' reliance on expensive purchased funds. Overall, the results are consistent with the hypothesis that foreign banks traded lower profits during the late 1980s and early 1990s in exchange for increased market share. The evidence implys an inability on the part of foreign-owned banks to develop the customer relationships necessary to raise and maintain core deposits – as a result, foreign-owned banks had to finance their explosive growth with a high-cost funding source. Additional study might determine whether foreign-owned banks began to close the efficiency gap during the 1990s (after their growth rates had slowed), or whether relative profit inefficiency varies by country of ownership.

References

Aguilar, Linda M. "A Current Look at Foreign Banking in the U.S. and Seventh District," *Economic Perspectives*, Federal Reserve Bank of Chicago, Vol. XIX, Issue 1, Jan./Feb. (1995).

Amel, Dean F. "State Laws Affecting the Geographic Expansion of Commercial Banks," Board of Governors of the Federal Reserve System, unpublished manuscript, August (1993).

Avery, Robert B., and Allen N. Berger, "Risk-Based Capital and Deposit Insurance Reform," *Journal of Banking and Finance* 15: 847-874 (1991).

Bank for International Settlements, "International Banking and Financial Market Developments." (various issues).

Bartholomew, Philip F., Helmut H.F. Binhammer, and Ralph Kolinski, "Canada and the United States: Will Financial Integration Work?" in James Barth and Philip F. Bartholomew (eds.), *Emerging Challenges for the International Financial Services Industry*, Greenwich, CT: JAI Press, 141-156 (1992).

Bartholomew, Philip F., and J. A. Galbraith, "U.S. and Canadian Deposit-Taking Institutions: Structure, Regulation and Inter-Country Relations," in William Milberg and Philip F. Bartholomew (eds.), *Prospects for Canadian-United States Economic Relations Under Free Trade*, Greenwich CT: JAI Press, 179-202 (1990).

Berger, Allen N., "Distribution-Free Estimates of Efficiency in the U.S. Banking Industry and Tests of the Standard Distributional Assumptions," *Journal of Productivity Analysis* 4: 261-292 (1993).

Berger, Allen N., Diana Hancock, and David B. Humphrey, "Bank Efficiency Derived from the Profit Function," *Journal of Banking and Finance*, 17: 317-347 (1993).

Berger, Allen N., William C. Hunter, and Stephen G. Timme, "The Efficiency of Financial Institutions: A Review and Preview of Research Past, Present, and Future," *Journal of Banking and Finance*, 17: 221-249 (1993).

Bleakley, Fred R., "U.S. Banks Lose Corporate Clients to Lenders Abroad," *Wall Street Journal*, September 29, 1992.

Budzeika, George, "Determinants of the Growth of Foreign Banking Assets in the United States," Federal Reserve Bank of New York, Research Paper No. 9112, May (1991).

Calomiris, Charles, and Mark Carey, "Loan Market Competition between Foreign and U.S. Banks: Some Facts about Loans and Borrowers," Federal Reserve Bank of Chicago, *Bank Structure and Competition*, May (1994).

Casson, Mark, "Evolution of Multinational Banks: A Theoretical Perspective," in Geoffrey Jones (ed.), *Banks as Multinationals*, London and New York: Routledge, 14-29 (1990).

The CBM Group, Inc., "Foreign Banks in America: Challenges and Opportunities," unpublished manuscript, New York (1995).

Chang, C. Edward, Iftekhar Hasan, and William C. Hunter, "Efficiency of Multinational Banks: An Empirical Investigation," unpublished manuscript, December (1994).

Cooper, S. Kerry, Donald R. Fraser, Peter S. Rose, Larry Wolken, "U.S. Activities of Pacific-Rim and European Banks: Evidence for a Global Integrated Market for Bank Credit?" *The Review of Research in Banking and Finance*, 1-25, Fall (1989).

Damanpour, Faramarz, "Global Banking: Developments in the Market Structure and Activities of Foreign Banks in the United States," *Columbia Journal of World Business*, Vol. 26, No. 3, Fall (1991).

DeYoung, Robert, "Determinants of Cost Efficiencies in Bank Mergers," Office of the Comptroller of the Currency, Economic & Policy Analysis Working Paper 93-1, Washington, DC, August (1993).

DeYoung, Robert, "Fee-Based Services and Cost Efficiency in Commercial Banks," *Proceedings: The Declining Role of Banks*, Federal Reserve Bank of Chicago, May: 501-519 (1994).

Elyasiani, Elyas, and Seyed Mehdian, "A Nonparametric Frontier Model of Internationally-Owned and Dometically-Owned Bank Cost Structures," unpublished manuscript, August 1993.

Federal Financial Institutions Examination Council, "Reports of Assets and Liabilities of U.S. Branches and Agencies of Foreign Banks."

_____, "Reports of Condition and Income."

Frankel, Allen B., and Paul B. Morgan, "Deregulation and Competition in Japanese Banking," Board of Governors of the Federal Reserve System, *Federal Reserve Bulletin*, Vol. 78, No. 18, August: 579-593 (1992).

Goldberg, Ellen S., "Comparative Cost Analysis of Foreign Owned U.S. Banks," *Journal of Bank Research*, Autumn (1982).

Goldberg, Lawrence G., "The Competitive Impact of Foreign Commercial Banks in the United States," in R. Alton Gilbert (ed.), *The Changing Market in Financial Services*, Boston/Dordrecht/London: Kluwer Academic Publishers (1992).

Goldberg, Lawrence G., and Robert Grosse. "Location Choice of Foreign Banks in the United States," *Journal of Economics and Business*, Vol. 46, No. 5, December (1994).

Goldberg, Lawrence G., and Anthony Saunders. "The Determinants of Foreign Banking Activity in the United States," *Journal of Banking and Finance*, Vol. 5, (1981).

Gray, H. Peter, and Jean Gray. "The Multinational Bank: A Financial MNC," *Journal of Banking and Finance*, Vol. 5, No. 1, March (1981).

Greenwich Associates, *The Coming Shift in Bank Relationships*, Greenwich, CT (1988).

_____, *Six Questions CFOs Might Ask Today*, Greenwich, CT (1992).

Grosse, Robert, and Lawrence G. Goldberg, "Foreign Bank Activity in the United States: An Analysis by Country of Origin," *Journal of Banking and Finance*, 15: 1093-1112 (1991).

Grubel, Herbert G. "A Theory of Multinational Banking," *Banca Nazionale del Lavoro Quarterly Review*, 123 (1977).

Houpt, James V., "International Trends for U.S. Banks and Banking Markets," Board of Governors of the Federal Reserve System Staff Study, Washington, DC, May (1988).

Hultman, W., and L. Randolph McGee, "Factors Affecting the Foreign Banking Presence in the U.S.," *Journal of Banking and Finance*, 13, 383-396 (1989).

Humphrey, David B., "Cost Dispersion and the Measurement of Economies in Banking," Federal Reserve Bank of Richmond, *Economic Review*, May: 24-38, 1987.

Hughes, Joseph P., and Loretta J. Mester, "Evidence on the Objectives of Bank Managers," *Proceedings: The Declining Role of Banks*, Federal Reserve Bank of Chicago, May: 496-500 (1994).

"International Competitiveness of U.S. Financial Institutions," *Hearings before the Subcommittee on Financial Institutions Supervision, Regulation and Insurance*, the House Committee on Banking, Finance and Urban Affairs, United States House of Representatives, March 21 and 22 (1990).

Jackson, William, "Foreign Banking in America: Growth and Regulation," *CRS Report for Congress*, Congressional Research Service, Library of Congress, June 8, 1993.

Key, Sydney J., and Gary M. Welsh, "Foreign Banks in the United States," in Baughn, William H., Thomas I. Storrs, and Charles E. Walker (editors), *The Bankers' Handbook*, third edition, Homewood, Illinois: Dow Jones-Irwin (1988).

Kraus, James R., "Foreign Banks Control 45% of Corporate Loans in U.S," *American Banker*, June 15, 1992.

_____, "Estimate of Foreign Bank Lending in U.S. Raised," *American Banker*, June 16, 1992.

_____, "Foreign Banks' Big Market Share Hides Weak Profits," *American Banker*, February 28, 1995.

LaFalce, John J., "Report of the Task Force on the International Competitiveness of U.S. Financial Institutions," Subcommittee on Financial Institutions Supervision, Regulation and Insurance, the House Committee on Banking, Finance and Urban Affairs, United States House of Representatives (1990).

Lund, David C., "Foreign Banking in the United States," U.S. Department of Commerce, *Foreign Direct Investment in the United States: An Update*, June: 40-50 (1993).

McCauley, Robert N., and Rama Seth, "Foreign Bank Credit to U.S. Corporations: The Implications of Offshore Loans," Federal Reserve Bank of New York, *Quarterly Review*, Spring: 52-65 (1992).

Mester, Loretta J., "Efficiency of Banks in the Third Federal Reserve District," Federal Reserve Bank of Philadelphia, Working Paper No. 94-1, December (1993).

Nolle, Daniel E., "Foreign Bank Operations in the United States: Cause for Concern?," in H. Peter Gray and Sandra C. Richard (eds.), *International Finance in the New World Order*, Oxford, England: Elsevier Science, Ltd. (1995).

Rugman, Alan M., and Shyan J. Kamath, "International Diversification and Multinational Banking," in Sarkis J. Khouri and Alo Ghosh (eds.), *Recent Developments in International Banking and Finance*, Vol. 1, D.C. Heath and Co. (1987).

Seth, Rama, "Profitability of Foreign Banks in the United States," Federal Reserve Bank of New York, Research Paper No. 9225, December (1992).

Seth, Rama, and Alicia Quijano, "Japanese Banks' Customers in the United States," Federal Reserve Bank of New York, *Quarterly Review*, Spring: 79-82 (1991).

_____, "Growth in Japanese Lending and Direct Investment in the United States: Are They Related?" *Japan and the World Economy*, 5: 363-372 (1993).

Swamy, P.A.V.B., Jalal D. Akhavein, and Stephen B. Taubman, "A General Method for Deriving the Efficiencies of Banks from a Profit Function," unpublished manuscript, April (1994).

Terrell, Henry S., "U.S. Branches and Agencies of Foreign Banks: A New Look," Board of Governors of the Federal Reserve System, *Federal Reserve Bulletin*, Vol. 79, No. 10. October: 913-925 (1993).

Wagster, John, Kerry Cooper, and James Kolari, "The Consequences of Regulatory Discretion in Implementing the Basle Accord: Capital Market Evidence," paper presented at the Eastern Finance Association Meetings. April (1994).

Zhu, Suzhen, Paul Ellinger, C. Richard Shumway, and David L. Neff, "Specification of Inefficiency in Banking: A Comparison of Cost and Profit Approaches," unpublished manuscript, April (1994).

Zimmer, Steven A., and Robert N. McCauley, "Bank Cost of Capital and International Competition," Federal Reserve Bank of New York, *Quarterly Review,* Winter: 33-59 (1991).

Zimmerman, Gary C., "Difficult Times for Japanese Agencies and Branches," Federal Reserve Bank of San Francisco, *Weekly Letter*, Number 93-26, October 22 (1993).

www.ingramcontent.com/pod-product-compliance
Lightning Source LLC
Chambersburg PA
CBHW081805170526
45167CB00008B/3329